REAL TALK

How to Say the Things You've Never
Said So You Can Get the Things
You've Always Wanted

Hilary Arnow Burns

REAL TALK: How to Say the Things You've Never Said So You Can Get the Things You've Always Wanted

By Hilary Arnow Burns

For permissions, email: hilary@gettingrealwithhilary.com

RealTalkWithHilary.com

Cover design: Rhianon Paige

Editing: Dustin Dixon

Printed in the United States

First Edition: 2023

ISBN: 979-8-218-17184-1

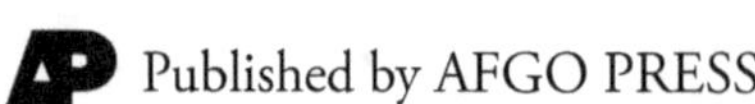 Published by AFGO PRESS

TABLE OF CONTENTS

A NOTE TO YOU, DEAR READER

In the coming pages, I will refer to what I call the "Getting Real Process" and how it improves one's chances of living a joyful and purposeful life without apology, shame, or regret.

To better understand how you may be subconsciously stifling, blaming, and otherwise sabotaging yourself, I invite you to go to www.RealTalkwithHilary.com and download my eye-opening "Real Talk Quiz" It's free (and fun!), and it may turn out to be the impetus you need to put an end to your unnecessary suffering.

With love and belief in you,
Hilary Arnow Burns

March 2023

INTRODUCTION

My Husband Wouldn't Have Sex With Me

The pain rose to the surface like an unstoppable tide. I began sobbing so hard that the hairdresser's chair shook. Debbie, who hadn't even touched my hair yet, looked at me, aghast. "Don't worry; I can fix those roots."

"It's not my hair," I cried. "It's my husband. He won't have sex with me."

What happened next became the catalyst for all the good things that would (eventually) start to happen in my life, and it was all because my conversation with Debbie forced me to, in effect, start talking and get real.

I was about to turn 50. My husband wasn't at all interested in me romantically. Our finances constantly stressed me out. He loved to borrow money, and I hated debt. We had no quality time as he was always off with my son at hockey games or any number of other activities.

I was *almost* happy a few years before when I was naive enough to think that my only problem was the baby weight I hadn't lost after my pregnancies. My kids were 12 and 14, so obviously, this wasn't a new thing. It seemed like an easy solution to me; lose the weight. Then I could *finally* be happy.

But it turns out I was numbing myself by eating and drinking. Once I started losing the weight and keeping it off, I became aware of emotions I wasn't familiar with. I hadn't allowed myself to feel things like sadness, frustration, anger, and disappointment. So instead of continuing to numb myself, I decided to "get real" about the fact that *I didn't like my life* and I was desperately unhappy with how things were. It was hard to admit because, unlike weight loss, there was no easy solution here.

I started wondering what had happened to me and my life. I attended a high school reunion and had another "get real" moment.

"Hils," my friend Dave yelled. "It's so great to see you! Remember how much fun we had together in high school?"

"Fun?" I questioned. "I was fun?"

Driving home that night, I wondered where the confident, popular, successful Hilary had gone. I became determined to find her and get my real life back. The life I loved. The one where I respected, valued, and cared for myself — the one where I looked forward to each day.

Let me give you a little background: When I got married,

I thought I was marrying my best friend. Sometime after marriage, my husband stopped listening to me. He did what he wanted. I went along with it.

I thought my job was to stay married by keeping my husband happy. You didn't ask for anything; the man was the boss. My mother didn't complain, so I didn't think I should. I thought I was supposed to be positive, no matter what. My role was to respect my husband. So I stayed quiet.

To make it worse, whenever I summoned the courage to speak up to my husband in front of my mother, she would yell, "Stop it, stop it." She wanted me to keep *him* happy by keeping my mouth shut and going along with whatever he wanted. She always took his side, making me feel like I was in the wrong.

It made me feel isolated.

I didn't have much going on in the way of self-worth. If I asked my husband how he would pay for what he'd just bought, he would turn the conversation against me and tell me I was always upset.

I believed my unhappiness was my fault. I had forgotten everything good about myself and thought I was just a miserable, bitter, crazy person.

At some point, the debt that my husband had accumulated started getting to me. I decided to try to fix it myself. I tried making budgets and monitoring our spending, but ultimately I couldn't control my husband's spending. We got further and further into debt. It didn't bother him, however. He just thought I was crazy to worry. "What is the problem?" he would ask.

"I don't like debt," I would say. "Can we monitor what we are spending?"

"Sure," he would respond. "I will check with you before I spend. No problem."

This conversation would always occur on Sundays, the start of a new week.

But when Tuesday came, and I saw him buying things, I lost it.

"You promised," I would yell. "You said you would check with me before spending money."

"I never promised that. I would never say those words. You are nuts. You are always upset about something. You are the most upset person I know."

I started thinking maybe it was me, that I really was crazy. Maybe there was something wrong with me. Was I *always* upset? Was I *always* like this?

I'd never heard of gaslighting before, but if I had, I'd recognize his comments as attempts to control me by making me believe I was crazy.

When I asked him about our sex life, it was the same thing.

"Tonight, we will have sex." And then that night, "Maybe tomorrow."

Finally, one day, he told me it just "didn't occur to him" to have sex with me.

I felt as though I'd been stabbed in the heart. Was I that unattractive?

Was there something genuinely *wrong* with me?

And there was our relationship or lack thereof. He was always off with my son at hockey games.

"Well, you're welcome to come with us," he would say cheerfully, oblivious to my complete lack of interest.

I had so much resentment toward hockey that that was the last thing I wanted to do. Again, I asked myself, "Is there something wrong with me? Should I *want* to go to these hockey games?"

Until that day at the hairdresser's, I thought everything was my fault, that maybe I was deeply flawed, and this was as good as life would get.

As you can imagine, I didn't feel great about myself or my life.

That day at the hairdresser's, I started talking "by accident." What I mean is that I started saying things I wouldn't usually say to anyone. But this day was different. When Debbie asked me how I was, instead of clamming up, I started crying… and then *talking*.

"What's going on?" she asked.

I blurted out the part about our sex life; "I know it's my fault that we don't have sex."

"WHAT? No, it's not," she interrupted. "Guys like sex. If your husband doesn't want sex, that's his problem, not yours. Michael," she said to her boyfriend, who was folding towels, "have you ever said no to sex?"

"No,' he said. "No, never."

"See, it's not you. It's his problem. Guys like sex."

Ok, so my hairdresser had a pretty narrow view of men. Of course, I knew it was much more complicated than that, but at the time, I was so sick of blaming myself that I welcomed the opportunity to blame him.

Then again, realizing that maybe it wasn't all my fault was a relief. If, somehow, he was also a part of the problem, then maybe, just maybe, I could stop blaming myself for *everything*.

I could be kinder to myself. Maybe I could learn to stand up for myself.

For the first time in a very long time, I saw a glimmer of hope that there might be a life I could enjoy living.

And who knows, maybe I could find someone who wanted

to have sex with me, someone who didn't think he was doing me a favor by patting me on the head and saying, *"Maybe tonight."*

What I had thought was the truth, that the problems in my marriage were all my fault, wasn't necessarily true at all. By saying how I felt *out loud,* something I never dared to do before (because keeping my mouth shut was a rule I was taught to obey), something in me opened up. I began to question my thinking.

Now, you may be wondering, *What's your responsibility in all of this, Hilary?*

I'll admit, I didn't know enough to ask myself that question, let alone answer it. But the revelation that it wasn't all my fault was enough to get me started.

What I came to realize is that we grow and mature in stages. Stage 1 is about saying unspoken things out loud – the things we're afraid to say – to someone actually willing to listen without judgment.

In order to create the life you long for (and get the things you've always wanted), you must first be willing to GET REAL and say the things you've never said. If you allow them to stay inside you, they will continue to suck the life out of you.

Only then can you look at your thinking, poke holes in your assumptions, and create a new thought model that gets you what you want. You see, without saying it out loud, you never really *hear* the thoughts running through your mind, spinning the same things over and over. You end up feeling crazier and crazier and more and more out of control.

Have you ever had that feeling?

The second time I spoke up was also by accident, meaning I never intended to allow the unspoken words out of my mouth. I was having lunch with some friends, something I rarely did because I didn't want to spend the money. They were discussing things like renovations and vacations. Things I couldn't relate to.

When they asked me how I was, the tears sprang forth unabated. I was no longer able to contain my real feelings. They were now on display for everyone to see.

I spilled it all out. I told my friends about my husband's spending, how our finances left me feeling scared half the time, and how I no longer had a sex life because *my husband had no interest in having sex with me!*

They listened. They didn't judge. They asked questions and offered a few suggestions, but mostly, they bore witness to my pain *without making me feel bad about feeling bad.*

I realized I wasn't alone; I no longer had to isolate myself. I had friends who didn't condemn me for my feelings, and the best part was that there was something I could do about my situation.

I started shifting how I saw my circumstances. Over time,

I started talking to more people, and gradually, I began to change.

I started feeling happy.

I gave much thought to why this was happening and came to realize that the shift in me was caused by four radical steps I took, intuitively, to turn my life around. I call it my **Getting Real Process,** and it taught me how to say the things I always wanted to say (but was too afraid to speak up) so that I could ultimately have the things I always wanted.

I woke up to the fact that nothing had worked before because I was operating on the belief that it was all my responsibility to make things better. However, the way I took responsibility still left me feeling unfulfilled.

For example, I thought my husband had to change *so I could be happy.* I thought if he didn't change, there was no choice but for me to feel stuck with the life I had. Since I couldn't change him (as if I ever really could have), I was a failure at that, too.

This *seemed* like the truth until I started saying the unspoken things out loud.

When we don't challenge our thoughts, we risk allowing them to run our lives. Once I got free of my thinking, anything became possible.

It didn't happen overnight, but it made such a profound impact on me that I wanted to share it with others.

The Getting Real Process (GRP) isn't necessarily easy. It takes courage. It requires you to say what you don't think you can or should.

We are taught not to be negative, complain, or be "high maintenance." The **GRP** undoes this unrealistic line of thinking. It demands that we "get real" by speaking up and *saying* what's really going on in our minds.

It takes courage to say the unpleasant stuff. But that is how we set ourselves free to create the life we truly desire.

You may have already taken many courses, read books, and done some personal inner work. I did too. The problem was that they didn't have long-lasting results. They focused on *doing* things differently, not *seeing* things differently.

And another thing: I believed I had to fix myself. I thought something was wrong with me and that all my problems were my fault. The only thing that needed to be corrected was my perspective.

The **GRP** approach is different from all the typical advice out there. That's because it starts with self-acceptance and allowing **"Real Talk"** to come out of your mouth, without self-blame, without self-judgment.

This simple act of speaking out loud is the first step toward freedom.

Real Talk releases everything you have always been afraid to say (or don't even know there is to say).

It's the only way you can ever begin to set yourself free.

When you find a safe space to say *anything*, you begin to see those invisible barriers you didn't even know existed. I'm not talking about blurting things out irresponsibly; I'm talking about releasing years of pain by *talking about that pain* out loud.

Next, we go to work building new, empowering, joyful contexts for your life. It takes courage and persistence to overcome resistance, fear, and self-judgment. But it's also fun, freeing, and allows you to embrace yourself and your life.

You become the magician in your own magical life.

I learned from the bible that God doesn't create junk, which meant I could embrace my "flaws" and my gifts. I saw that the story I had made up about myself and my life just wasn't true.

I can tell myself *any* story. Why not tell an empowering one that helps me create the life I always wanted?

I am happy to report that I have done just that. I have created a new reality and a life I love instead of the one I *thought* I was doomed to live.

I created this program because I realized there are others who think they are stuck in a certain way of living with no way out. If that's you, please know that if you are willing to be open and consider that your thoughts about the circumstances of your life may be false, things really can change.

Without giving yourself the gift of **Real Talk,** you risk staying exactly where you are, feeling like you are missing out on something in life. And you would be absolutely right. You'd miss an opportunity to look at what might not be working and adjust accordingly so you could create a life full of passion, fun, love, and joy.

Imagine if you could communicate all the ways you feel dissatisfied in your life without recrimination. What if you stopped hiding how you felt about your body, your sex life, and your relationships with friends and family? What if you could give voice to how you feel about your living space?

What if you could simply declare, *out loud,* "I am not happy"?

I call it "getting off mute." By talking out loud about how you feel about the things that matter to you, you reveal yourself to YOU.

And with love and self-compassion, you can decide how much of what's going on in your own mind actually makes sense or if it's only making you suffer.

GETTING *MORE* REAL

Here's what happened after I started my Real Talk. I took control of my finances. I stopped listening to thoughts telling me I was disloyal to my husband by opening my own savings account. I began resolving my debt issues and started saving again. Eventually, I turned around my finances.

My energy improved. I had a newfound sense of vitality.

I started doing things I enjoyed again - Zumba, step classes, going to the library, and writing poems.

I even did a triathlon.

I soon began teaching clients the same process that had worked so well for me. After years of "wanting to but never doing it," they spoke up and then took action. One is opening a yoga studio, another is continuing to write her book, and one started conversations with her husband about what wasn't working. Their energy shifted from resignation and powerlessness to hope and joy. It has been nothing short of incredible.

When you say what you don't think you can say, without worrying about looking good, stupid, or crazy, with people you can trust to create a no-judgment zone for you, a whole new world opens up.

Your problems seem to lose their power over you.

The pieces get dislodged one by one, and you step into a vast open space that allows you to recreate the life of your dreams. Imagine a life where you can speak freely, dislodge your pain, and get the things you have always wanted.

How does that sound? *Saying what you've always been afraid to say* is your ticket to freedom.

Hop aboard.

THE GETTING REAL PROCESS

Let's *get real* for a moment.

Are you living the life you dreamed of having as a child or young adult? Is this how you thought your life would be?

If it were possible to get yourself free, would you be willing to go for it?

You might be going along every day saying you are fine; "This is just what life looks like. I was in a fantasy life when I was young. This is reality."

Or, you might say that life sucks, and then you die, that you have no control or say over how your life goes. You are stuck with your choices and can do nothing about it.

I'm going to show you how to get real about the life you are living by starting to talk out loud, without shame, and without feeling like a victim of your circumstances.

If you want to take your power back, you **must** speak up.

Since I decided to get real with myself, my life has been much more fulfilling. I used to feel powerless about my marriage, finances, and sex life. Then one day, I *said* it. I admitted I wasn't happy. That allowed me to *see* what was going on inside my own head and correct the thoughts that only served to sabotage me. Only then could I dream about the life I wanted without thinking I couldn't have it.

Instead, I took action to make it all happen.

I no longer feel like a confused victim, blaming myself and my husband for everything that went wrong in my life. I got my power back, saw the actions to take, and started moving in that direction instead of staying stuck. I addressed each area of my life that wasn't working: I reversed my financial situation, funded my retirement, and rekindled my sex life. Some of my decisions were not easy, but you will hear more about them later. I am now living the dreams I had buried for all those years. I am excited about life and the possibilities that the future holds.

I just returned from a first-class trip to Panama with 255 friends. A trip like this was simply impossible before putting myself through the **Getting Real Process.** I never went on vacations. I was trying to turn my finances around and wouldn't allow myself to spend money. Once I regained my power, I could take steps to reverse my financial situation and save for vacations. I started looking for people who could grow, develop and live fully.

These were the people I went on vacation with — the kind of people I liked to be around.

The missing link had always been the need to address my flawed thinking. I was stuck blaming myself and trying the same things repeatedly, which is the definition of insanity. I had bought into thinking that I *knew* how my life would go. I listened to my negative thinking and thought it was the truth. I was afraid to speak out because I didn't want to be seen as a complainer (as my mother would say).

Then I woke up. Because of my hairdresser, no less. And that's when my perspective started to shift.

For the first time, I saw that by saying things out loud, I could see how my thinking kept me stuck instead of allowing me to dream again and take action.

The first step – SAY IT – is usually a profound moment. Just saying how you feel out loud can lead to massive revelations. Fortunately, I could return the favor to my hairdresser not long after I had created my **Getting Real Process.**

During my last hair coloring appointment, she was thoroughly agitated.

"You're just the person I need to talk to," she said. "I can't talk about this with anyone else. My family wants me to go to Italy with them. Last time I chickened out and didn't go. I can't tell them how I feel because they think I'm crazy. I'm terrified to fly. The last time I flew, back in 1986, there was terrible turbulence. I thought I was going to die. When I got off the plane, I vowed to myself that I would never fly again. I'm also afraid of getting sick over there. What will I do so far from home? I can't talk to my brother who wants me to go because he just doesn't understand."

We talked for a while. I asked some questions.

"Are you willing to revoke your promise to yourself that you will never fly again?"

She answered yes.

"Do you think they have hospitals and doctors in Italy that could treat you if you get sick?"

"Yes, I guess," she said.

By the end of our conversation, she was calm and even began dreaming about seeing her Italian relatives again and looking forward to it. I took her through the entire **Getting Real Process.** She could speak freely because she knew **Real Talk** was safe with me, that I wouldn't judge her or think she was nuts. By the end of my hair appointment, she was excited about her trip to Italy. No more worry or anxiety.

It was heartwarming to experience this transformation in her in the time it took to do my hair!

Until she started speaking out loud, she remained stuck in her thinking. She kept listening to the voice in her head and was afraid to say it aloud. That voice *seemed* real.

She discovered the difference between the voice in her head and what was actually happening in real life. We believe what we think, we keep quiet, and we live our lives accordingly. We can't see that we have any choice or power over how life can go. So we try to make the best of it, having pity parties to provide some excitement. That was as good as it got for me.

I used to tell myself it was fine, that I shouldn't be a dreamer. It's just the way it goes.

I couldn't have been more wrong.

If you're thinking (like I used to) and feeling hopeless or stuck, you are now in the right place. There is nothing wrong with you. We were conditioned as children to conform, be nice, don't rock the boat, and other cliches. We weren't taught how to figure out what we wanted, let alone ask for it.

This is for women who are tired of feeling bad about themselves; women who have put up with their disempowering thinking for too long; women who have listened to others bad-mouth them and not only believed what they heard but that it was wrong to speak up.

This is for women who are ready to regain their power and start finding joy, passion, and happiness again.

Oh, and by the way, this isn't just "positive thinking." Our mothers and relatives trained us to lay low and not cause a fuss. "Think positive," they would say.

With the Getting Real Process, we speak up, removing the shackles of the rules and regulations we have inherited and abided by for far too long.

Four steps make up the foundation of my **Getting Real Process,** which goes like this:

Step 1: SAY IT. I started getting my thoughts out of my head by talking *out loud* instead of stifling myself.

Step 2: SEE IT. I began to see what was happening in my mind and could then begin to poke holes in my own thinking.

Step 3: DREAM IT. Next, I could get in touch with what I wanted out of life instead of organizing myself around other people's dreams.

Step 4: DO IT. Only then would I be able to identify the action steps I could take to start going in the direction of MY dreams. I created the life I wanted instead of the life I thought I was stuck with (and settling for).

Before I came up with this process, I kept going back and forth between two ineffective strategies:

1. Try to get my husband to change.
2. Accept my fate and realize this was my lot in life.

When I focused on implementing Option #1, I did everything I could think of to fix my relationship; I read books, took courses, and set goals. Then, I tried working with my husband to change him and the situation.

When nothing worked, I resigned myself to becoming a victim of my reality. Hardly a strategy.

It's ok to say the negative things out loud. It's ok not to feel happy. It's ok to talk badly about what is going on. You will be encouraged to do this instead of being rebuked. What you say will be validated. And when ALL is finally said (even if not necessarily DONE), when you accept yourself as you are, without apology, miracles will start to happen, and you will be set **free**.

In Step 1, you are encouraged to "puke it all out."

We never learned how to do this in life. It takes strength and determination, but there is no judgment here. It's imperative to get all the gunk out. Then, we examine what you've said, decide which parts of what you are saying are YOUR truth, and discard the assumptions that have caused you to suffer. Gloria Steinem is famous for saying, "The truth will set you free, but first, it will piss you off."

Before moving on to the next steps, you must first learn how to say it out loud. The other steps depend on it.

Until you SAY IT, you won't be able to SEE IT.

If you can't see it, then you won't be able to DREAM IT.

And if you can't dream it, how are you ever supposed to DO IT (live your dream)?

Are you ready to get real with yourself and start living the life you *really* want?

Here we go…

STEP ONE

Say It

If you're reading this, I want to congratulate you on finding the courage to begin making changes in your life. This first step is about acknowledging that there are things you'd like to change.

Without saying what is in your mind, you are attempting to problem-solve without knowing what problem you are trying to solve. It's like putting icing on a mud pie. You can try and try to change things without this step, but you will just end up back where you are because you have not examined your limiting beliefs. By saying your thoughts out loud, by admitting your feelings, your fears, and your endless worries, you get it all out of your head.

The **Getting Real Process** gives you freedom right from its very first step.

In order to prepare for this step, you will need to be tired of feeling like:

> » There's no hope of communication in your marriage or relationship.

» You'll never enjoy your life again, and you don't know what happened to it.

» Your finances suck, and that's just the way it is.

» You are fine doing nothing because "What's the point"?

» You're ok never having sex again; "It's overrated anyway."

You're just tired of feeling this resignation, heaviness, despair, and hopelessness over these or similar issues.

It's important in this step to have compassion for yourself and the willingness to be honest, courageous, and free to really express how it's been. You will need to trust that this isn't the time to worry about "how it looks." Raw naked honesty is vital in this step. The toughest part is to let your thoughts, feelings, opinions, and shame emerge. Otherwise, they will still be inside of you, sabotaging your efforts.

I invite you to let go of the notion that you can't say how it really is for you, that there is something wrong with how you *honestly* feel. Practice saying some of the unspoken rules, cliches, opinions, comments, criticisms, and insults that are running your life, even if only to yourself at first. By telling your story, you get it all out of your head so you can take it apart in the next step.

We tend to live inside a box of our own creation that is invisible to us. We don't even know we are stuck in the box. This exercise gets us talking so we can identify some of the walls that keep us trapped. It is essential to keep talking until there is nothing left to say.

For a long time, I was ashamed of how I looked. My father had told me he was ashamed to look at me. I thought something was wrong with me until I finally started talking about it. Someone told me this was not my problem but my father's. He had personal issues regarding people's weight. I shouldn't have had to take that on. I was only a few pounds heavier than I used to be. I started accepting myself and loving myself as I am. This helped me to let go of the shame.

Without having a safe place to talk about what we are thinking and feeling, we live like our negative thinking is true. Sometimes voicing our deepest fears, pulling them up to the surface, and then holding them to the light of day lets us see that they aren't as scary as we thought.

When we make ourselves wrong for being who we are or what we've done, we feel trapped. It's like saying we "should" be another way. Using the "should" word creates the trap. We stay trapped where we are until we become aware of what we are saying about ourselves and our lives.

Somehow, whenever I decide my body or finances should not be how they are, they worsen - I start eating or spending more. But when I can accept myself as I am, I can choose my actions freely without the pressure of my thinking.

Do you ever feel ashamed about what you think is wrong with you or something you may have done? Do you hide your authentic self? Are you a people-pleasing, "pleasant person" who thinks your job is to keep people happy? Do you go out of your way to avoid being criticized?

What makes it difficult is our thinking that if we say how we are REALLY feeling, no one will understand. We think we are the only person who feels this way. Somehow we believe all of this is our own fault and that we shouldn't bother people with our complaining.

I thought I had to be happy before I talked to people. I stayed by myself, hoping the negativity would pass. I used to call in sick from work if I felt especially awful. I didn't want anyone to see me that way.

We aren't aware that starting to speak out loud will lead to freedom. We think we are the only ones who feel this way, so we stay silent in order to hide our "real, shameful" selves. We are afraid that if people find out how we "really" are, they won't like us and will leave us. So it seems better to hide the part of us that makes us feel shame.

If you can relate, I have great news! You now have an opportunity to change all this.

You are not alone. Others have felt the same way and still managed to escape the trap and are now joyful, happy, and excited about life. You can learn *not* to be ashamed of how you think and feel. You don't deserve to stay miserable and powerless.

It's scary to tell people things that are in your head. I was afraid they would think I was seriously flawed. But that wasn't the case at all. Once I started talking, I realized that I wasn't alone. There were people who cared about me. They always had. I had just been hiding.

However, we need a judgment-free safe place to communicate whatever it is we need to say.

When I work with clients, I am always encouraging them to get it ALL out. No matter how long it takes. No matter how ugly it gets.

You might think that you can't do this or that you are unique in your unhappiness.

Silence is a pandemic.

Isn't it time to "get off mute?"

People are always grateful that I encouraged them to start talking (and to keep talking). I don't know anyone who was ever sorry they did. The reason people fear "saying too much" is that they think it might be used against them at some point.

To ensure you can trust the person you're talking to, test the waters. Say something and see how they respond. Are they empathetic? Do they care to help? Do they want to listen?

My **Getting Real Process** considers that you might be afraid and that self-doubt tries to keep you in check. I understand. It is a normal part of stepping into new territory. Having these feelings isn't wrong. It doesn't have to stop you. You can keep going despite the fear.

When people begin implementing Step 1 of my Process, they feel free. Their concerns, thoughts, and experiences are validated, perhaps for the first time in their lives.

They realize it doesn't always sound as bad as it is in their minds. They stop blaming themselves and thinking that there is something inherently flawed within them. They get excited and hopeful for the first time in a long time. They start to like **"Real Talk."**

Now that you have started talking and telling your story let's begin to poke some holes in it. You will see them for yourself the more you start talking. You will realize that sometimes things are much less scary in the real world than they can be in your mind.

It's time to see these things for what they truly are.

STEP TWO

See It

Now that you've gotten all that stuff out of your head, you can begin to SEE what you've been holding onto. You can question what you've said out loud to see whether it's true. Then we can begin poking holes in your story.

It might not be obvious, but the plot holes reveal themselves more and more as you go. We don't do it in a way that makes you feel bad. There's nothing wrong with thinking or feeling like you do. But I've found that once you can see these "holes," life opens up dramatically.

Essentially, we examine what you said in Step 1, challenge it, and see what is real vs. made up.

How much of your story is based on fact? How much of it is opinion?

One of the things that took me the longest to see was my incorrect belief that, somehow, our financial situation was my fault. I thought that, given my business degree, I should have been able to reverse the direction we were going in.

I finally saw that I was kidding myself to think I could control or change my husband. Why should he have to change just because I didn't like something?

He shouldn't. But what set me free was realizing that I didn't have to put up with how he did finances, sex, or relationships anymore. It wasn't working for me. He didn't have to change, but I also didn't have to do this anymore. It took a lot of courage and self-inquiry. I had a choice - stay as it was and accept things as they were, or leave. I made the difficult decision to leave and eventually got divorced. I'm not saying this is the right decision for everyone, but for me, it was. In order to have the life I wanted and dreamed of, I needed to be responsible for my life and take steps toward the life I wanted.

And so I did.

Step 2 is important because you start challenging what you had always assumed was true. Here are some examples:

> » Kaley just assumed that something was wrong with her because she kept saying she would get started with her business but never did. She thought that meant she was flawed in some way.

> » Barbara thought she would be poor forever, barely able to pay her bills in retirement.

> » Deirdre was so mad at her ex-husband that she couldn't move on. She believed the horrible things he had said about her and felt terrible about herself.

» Emily needed clarification about her career. She called herself unorganized and overwhelmed, and it prevented her from seeing clearly and taking any steps to make money.

When the bank in which I opened my private account, unbeknownst to me, sent a bank statement to my house, my husband started yelling at me. He wanted to take the money that *I had saved* and use it himself. I changed banks that day and would not let him take that money.

Believe me, it was hard to stand up to him.

He was a lawyer and very good at arguing. He insulted and threatened me, but I stood firm. I would no longer let him bully me and tell me I didn't know what I was doing. By remembering that I was good with money, intelligent, and a business school graduate, I took back the confidence I had let him steal from me. This moment was crucial for me to create the life I WANTED rather than perpetuating the life he wanted, the one that ignored my wants and needs.

Maybe you've tried everything you've known to do and are giving up. Perhaps you think I don't understand your circumstances. You don't have to believe me. But I hope you will at least consider that what I'm saying might be even a little bit true.

It all depends on what you think hurts more, "getting real" or staying stuck.

I don't know if I would have believed myself, either. When you feel like a victim, sometimes you don't want someone to help you because you are invested in feeling bad. If that's the case, maybe this is not the right time for you to get free. But can you at least consider what is being suggested here?

"It's just a bunch of happy horse shit," I might've said.

Ironically, I realized the horse shit was what I had been telling myself. That's when I decided to make some changes.

What if I *could* have what I wanted? Was it not worth suspending my disbelief and resignation to at least try? I had nothing to lose.

This step may still seem too hard. After all, you've been telling the same story for years. Maybe it gets you sympathy and makes others feel sorry for you. But is that *really* how you want to see yourself? Do you REALLY want to stay a victim that people feel sorry for? I was only ready when I was tired of being talked down to and patronized.

There might be some fear that your friends and family will feel threatened if you are happy and take your power back. Is their happiness more important than yours? Do you think you are deserving of a life you love? I think you are, but it doesn't matter what I think.

So what do you honestly think about your life, and how will you live it from this day forward?

Also, some people might prefer you to stay in the victim role. They are used to having the upper hand and having you be malleable. It might be uncomfortable for you to suddenly show up differently.

Are you ready for that?

Step 2 has you challenge the status quo and your current beliefs. People might have insulted you, and you accepted their insults. Accepting that you've been mistreated and done nothing about it may be difficult. But you can do something about it now!

My husband used to tell me I was "always upset." I was the most upset person he knew. After a while, I thought he was right. There was something wrong with me because of it. But after I poked holes in my story (and his), I saw that the things upsetting me were legitimate. I didn't like our marriage or that he didn't listen to me. Of course, that was upsetting!

I no longer let him accuse me of being upset, as if I had no right to feel that way. I had poked a hole in that one and released all of the wool he was trying to pull over my eyes. If you take your power back, is it possible you will be an even better mom, wife, daughter, sister, or employee? Might you even *elevate* the lives of everyone around you?

The answer is **YES.**

If your current mindset centers around blame, resignation, and victimization, it's next to impossible for you to chase your dreams. You probably wouldn't dare, am I right? In other words, it makes complete sense that you *feel* stuck. Your mind is set on "stuck." No wonder you feel helpless.

You may even think it's up to other people to fix things for you. But now, after Step 2, I hope you will at least consider that it's your thinking that is keeping you from your dreams.

I've worked with many women who felt terrible and just accepted it. When they started telling their story, they got to see which parts were real and which weren't.

One woman had given up and was looking for a place to die.

But once she started poking holes in her story, she became excited about living again.

Another woman had put off starting her yoga studio for three years. After we worked together, she put on an event with a 200% increase in attendance. She is now opening her studio.

Do you long for a life where you feel loved, are passionate about what you do, find joy in doing what you love, and are around people who love you? You don't have that now because (and I say this with all the compassion in my heart) you are too focused on your misery.

You look at the world through a window of shame and can't see beyond it.

Ready to do some window cleaning?

Once you have told your story and can begin to see the holes in it, you are ready to start dreaming again. Don't worry if you have some lingering doubt about whether you can do this; that is normal. But hundreds of women before you have done it. So dust off those old hopes and aspirations, and let's get going.

Now it's your turn.

STEP THREE

Dream It

Do you keep your dreams to yourself?

Or do you dream them out loud as declarations of how you intend to live your life?

"I want to have a show," I said, "where people tell their stories, get to know what's great about themselves, and inspire others. I want to be an inspiring storyteller, too!"

I was excited for about 5 seconds.

"You can't do that," my mind shot back. "You don't know how to do that. Don't get your hopes up; you'll just be disappointed. Again. Besides, what will people think? You'll embarrass yourself." Those were the thoughts that threatened my dream. Those thoughts seemed to be the truth.

And yours may seem like the truth too. You may believe you have "real" reasons why your dreams can't ever come true.

But here's the thing; when we allow our thoughts to be spoken out loud, it can be hard not to laugh at the stuff that comes out of our mouths.

Step 3 is connected to steps 1 and 2 because you can't develop what you want while still in your victim story. So in step 2, we poke holes in your thinking until you are ready to see out of your dark place and connect to the light.

Without all three steps, you are just staying in the same story. What happens if you miss a step or two on a flight of stairs? You fall down. We need all three steps to gradually take apart your reality so we can create a new one.

Without all three steps, I would have just stayed a victim, envious and resigned. I probably wouldn't have had the conversations I had because I was too ashamed of my situation. I wouldn't have gotten clear about what I wanted, seen what could stop me, come up with an action I could take, and then taken it.

You might be skeptical at the ease of how I reversed my situation. I would be too. But here's the thing; it didn't happen overnight.

It took a while for me to start saying things out loud. It took time for me to see the holes in my story. I didn't have anyone guiding me through this process because the process didn't exist. I created it by accident as I was going through the fire.

Today I am guiding, validating, and walking women through the **Getting Real Process.** I honor and accept them as they are, helping them see the holes in their (old) stories so they can finally release the shame that has kept them stuck for years.

We have to be willing to be *real,* honest, and *wrong* about our current beliefs about our lives. Then, we must be ready to dig deep and say what needs to be said. We must allow our objections to surface and get them out "on paper." This takes courage and a willingness to make sacrifices in order to create a life we love and deserve.

Before I could start dreaming of a new reality, I had to shed other people's judgments about how I should be. I had to shed the thought that no one wanted to hear what I had to say and that it was wrong to say it. It's not changing so much as accepting yourself exactly as you are instead of how others think you should be.

I had to stop blaming myself, feeling hopeless, playing the victim, and being willing to be wrong about my situation. I had to stop blaming others for my problems and take responsibility for my own life. I had to be willing to say that I wanted the finances I had when I was single. To admit that the way I was living was no longer tolerable. It wasn't comfortable or easy, but it was worth it.

I am finally living the life of my dreams, and I hope that you will too.

To start defining your dream, you have to be willing to first go through Steps 1 and 2. Then, when the cobwebs have been removed, you will start to remember what you once dared to dream. Will you have the courage to speak your dreams out loud, even if you are shy or embarrassed?

Immediately, all the reasons you can't have your dreams will pop into your head:

> » Don't be ridiculous - you can't have that!

> » You sound stupid - just stop talking!

» You know you tried that before; just stop.

» What will people think?

And on and on and on. Step 3 brings you face-to-face with your dreams. We allow them to rise to the surface so we can get to know them once again.

Notice, there is nothing to *do* yet. We are busy preparing our minds so that when we're ready to take action, our thoughts will propel us forward.

If you are tired of thinking that your life has to stay the way it is, ask yourself if you're ready to make some changes. Don't be afraid. We will start small. You won't have to stand up to bullies at the beginning. By the time that happens, if it does, you will already be stronger and more confident.

Living your dream means taking on obstacles that may get in the way.

The **Getting Real Process** will help you start washing off the mud that has covered you up in the form of negative thoughts and beliefs. When you start questioning them and creating new beliefs and realities about yourself and your life, you will blow your mind wide open.

You'll know you are making progress when you have moments of joy, can take a deep breath and smile, exercise some of your strengths and gifts, and start seeing the life you truly want, even if it's for short moments at first. It might disappear as soon as you see it, but those small glimpses of hope are how you know you are making progress. You will begin to have moments where you start thinking you CAN have a life you love.

Wouldn't that be fun?

Now that you have started speaking your truth out loud, poking holes in your story, defining what you want, and identifying what you think is in the way, we can create an action plan. In Step 4, we will identify small action steps you can take to get yourself on your way to a new life.

Don't worry; it won't be anything you can't handle. And rest assured that we're not going to "blow it all up" and create a big mess.

Still, you may feel some resistance. Remind yourself that resistance is an emotional barrier you must go through at your own pace.

Think of your resistance as an electric fence, the other side of which is the freedom you crave. What will you choose to do? Save yourself from the momentary zap and stay where you are? Or will you go through it, knowing the discomfort is temporary but well worth it in exchange for the freedom that awaits on the other side?

Time to break free!

STEP FOUR

Do It

Many of my clients are afraid to say what they really want because they are afraid to fail. They're afraid of messing it all up. What if you couldn't fail? What would you do in your life right now if you knew the outcome was guaranteed?

Years ago, I had set a date for when I wanted to hit a certain weight goal at Weight Watchers. I missed it for years. But it didn't matter. I just kept resetting the goal. I kept going. And one day, I hit my goal weight, kept it off for six weeks, and became a Lifetime member. I was so happy that I hadn't quit. It didn't matter that I didn't hit it when I thought I would. It was worth the frustration, persistence, and discipline to keep trying. That moment was incredibly gratifying.

In Step 4, we identify small goals to accomplish. We then break the goal down into bite-sized action steps that are doable — things like making a phone call, sending an email, or researching a class — tiny steps toward a bigger goal. As you take these steps, your energy, attitude, and focus will be altered in a profound way.

Each small win gives you the confidence to pursue another. It is contagious and ultimately makes you want to take more steps toward your goals and dreams.

If you haven't done Steps 1, 2, and 3, then Step 4 is not likely to stick. Taking action without experiencing the transformative powers of the previous steps could turn out to be futile.

When I would lose weight, I couldn't understand why I would put it right back on, *plus more* each time. I came to realize that it was because I hadn't done Step 1 (SAY IT), which would have allowed me to articulate *out loud* all the reasons why I was numbing myself with food. At the time, I didn't even know I was numbing myself. Step 1 would have allowed me to get out the crap that was in my way and GET REAL with some REAL TALK. I was still thinking I was "fine" and that *body weight* was my only problem.

Step 2 (SEE IT) would have then allowed me to examine what was bothering me and take a good hard look at what was *real* compared to what I had made up in my mind. I'm certain I would have gotten some freedom around my whole story about my life, my weight, and why I *thought* I was stuck and that there was nothing I could do.

Step 3 (DREAM IT) would have allowed me to get *present* to what I really wanted and how I had been the one to stand in the way of my dreams because I had made up so many reasons for why I couldn't have those things. Not until I was able to ditch the reasons (and the excuses) was I free to move on to Step 4, which is all about taking action.

Looking back, I could see how many times I would skip straight to taking action, bypassing the necessary *inner* work of Steps 1, 2, and 3.

While I'm sure you're curious to know what happens in Step 4, I caution you not to push yourself if you're not ready. By the way, "ready" makes you feel inspired to take action, unlike the feeling of deprivation I used to feel whenever I put myself "on a diet."

Step 4 is fun! We feel *motivated* to develop a plan. We break it down into small, doable steps. If you're unsure about how to do something, we break it down further until it is as simple as making a phone call. Or Googling something. Or putting away 5 things.

One of my clients wanted to learn the first 5 minutes of an exercise routine, and she was finding it very difficult. She felt overwhelmed and stuck and wanted to quit. In Step 4, we broke the routine down even further. She only had to commit to learning 20 seconds of the routine! She was elated. She was thrilled. She told everyone who would listen how excited she was.

And guess what? Not surprisingly, after the initial 20 seconds, she learned the next 20 seconds of the routine in way less time. It literally changed how she felt about herself, what she could accomplish, and how she saw life.

Whatever sets you free, right?

Now, if you get to Step 4 and aren't feeling free, you're likely to sabotage your efforts to take action toward change. Self-sabotage is a signal that there's more work to do in Steps 1, 2, and 3. Go back, do the work, and be persistent.

The payoff will come.

I had another client who was trying to learn a 5-minute comedy routine. She had little pieces of paper all around her house from notes from the coach she was paying to help her. She was stuck.

She didn't want to do the work to organize the paper, practice what she had been coached to do, and learn the routine. I worked with her to uncover what she *wasn't* saying. "I don't like it when someone tells me what to do. I don't want to do it."

We discussed the money she was paying her coach AND her dream of mastering comedy. She realized what was holding her back was an old belief that she "didn't like being told what to do."

With that, she got into action mode, learned the routine, and is now headlining for famous comedians in New York City. She tells me she is "forever grateful" for the **Getting Real Process.**

You see, once we dismantle the roadblocks that we have put up in front of our dreams, things start to happen.

Now, let's recap how the **Getting Real Process** works:

Step 1, SAY IT. Saying the things you never allowed yourself to say out loud can be very liberating. It can also be terrifying. Nevertheless, this is where you start because keeping it all locked up in your mind hasn't worked, has it? Get your story out of your head and on the table.

Next is **Step 2, SEE IT.** See what's going on in your mind and determine what is real (fact), what is made up, and what existing beliefs, rules, and limitations are in your way.

If you don't get real about your story, you'll continue to believe you can't have what you want.

You'll continue to NOT BELIEVE in your dreams.

Step 3, DREAM IT, requires us to identify what we really want and then clear out any old thoughts and beliefs that tell us we can't have it. Thought by thought, belief by belief, we dismantle them all. We don't stop until we *feel free.*

Step 4, DO IT. Finally, we can take the action we want to take, not because we feel we have to or because we'll feel guilty if we don't, but because we genuinely *want* to. Most goals fail when we go straight to Step 4 while dreading doing anything. A clean mental slate ensures you don't end up back where you started.

It's one thing to feel hopeless, defeated, and helpless from time to time; we're human, after all. Problems start to build when we can't handle our emotions, and we try to push through them with a "just do it" attitude. Unless you're playing sports, that won't cut it.

The **Getting Real Process** is a commitment to the highest version we have of ourselves.

Are you worth fighting for?

If you think you're incapable of getting real, it may be because you haven't met someone you can trust to hear what you have to say without experiencing a backlash.

Or maybe you are still worried about what people will think about you should you decide to say it out loud. You may think it's easier to keep smiling and nodding your head, even when you disagree with what's going on around you.

Or you may need to uphold a certain image of yourself to earn the approval of others.

Maybe you want to continue to do whatever you can to ward off rejection, failure, or disappointment.

But consider this: What is the cost of avoiding those emotions? What price do you have to pay to maintain the status quo?

Maintaining the status quo may have a substantial monetary cost. It may have a negative impact on your career. I remained stuck in my career until I poked holes in my story about how I couldn't have what I wanted. I even made myself sick in order to take some time alone when I felt especially bad.

My relationships suffered because I was miserable to be around.

Reclaiming our lives requires us to muster the inner strength we don't even know we have. Recognize the lingering resistance and ask yourself if the status quo is worth more than the promise of freedom.

I have many client testimonials about how my **Getting Real Process** helped them escape the status quo. They are now excited about life. They came into my program resigned and defeated but emerged connected, alive, and committed to a better future. They felt safe with me. They spoke their truth out loud.

This is why I love the work I do. I get to pay it forward.

My kids are very proud of my transformation. Instead of feeling sorry for me, they respect me and say that none of their friends have moms like me. They see me leaving my comfort zone and going beyond where I thought I could. So many other moms are working hard just to maintain the status quo. If only they knew there was another way.

The only boundary between you and the life of your dreams is, ironically, the fear of **Real Talk.** If you're afraid to be real and don't know what it is that makes you feel that way, at least say *that.*

There is no wrong thing you can ever say.

Everything you say deserves to be heard.

YOUR NEXT STEPS

I recently had a client call me, and oh boy, was she upset. She was away on holiday, and her husband was coming to spend time with her. She already knew how it would go (not well) and thought she would be better off alone.

During that call, she got to say *everything* she was thinking and feeling, what she feared would happen, and how she "knew" it would go. Then, I helped her poke holes in her story. After all, he hadn't even gotten there, and she was already afraid, irritated, and "better off alone."

Then, I asked her what she *did* want. She said she wanted to have fun and adventure and feel love when she was with him. That was her dream. Only then did we outline steps she could take to make that dream come true.

By asking her challenging questions and not buying into her perceived reality (her story), I got her to consider the possibility of an entirely different outcome. By giving up being "right" about her story, she got to experience freedom. But first, she had to be willing to believe that things *could* go differently. She really does love the guy and doesn't want to be alone. She was shocked when she realized the actual cost of sticking to her story, and she let it go.

This led to a long-lasting result.

After her husband's visit, she texted me: *"Thank you so much. Sam and I had the best ten days of our life. You are the best. Without our conversation, we may have ended up separating. Thank you again."*

I know, it seems too easy.

Guess what? It's not.

Yes, you will be uncomfortable telling the truth at first. You might not even know what the truth is.

But you won't be alone. I will be there for you! I love to help people get real and watch them set themselves free.

I realize you might be thinking, "This is all just a sales pitch." I get it. I've fallen for many pitches over the years. It makes one wary.

Salespeople are good at persuasion. Your skepticism may have saved you from having been "pitched." But at some point, we have to wonder if it hasn't also stopped us from seizing excellent opportunities.

You might think it's too late for you, or you've tried everything already. Well, that's what I thought too. But what I found is that the solution was not that tricky.

I was the one holding onto my flawed thinking. So when I decided the cost of being right was too high to hold onto, I started working on setting myself free. So what is the cost of being "right" about how you see things? What if it's your happiness?

The trouble with us humans is that we want guarantees, along with being right. We want to know for certain that something will work.

And yet, we don't want to commit to making it work, *no matter what.*

I'm not promising you a cure. This is a roadmap to the life of your dreams. It shows you the way, but you must steer yourself in the right direction. No one can do it for you.

At this point, you could go in a few different directions. You could:

Option 1. Do nothing and stay where you are. You've lived this way a long time and survived. But seeing as you've read this far, I'll assume that you've decided you want to change.

Option 2. Do it yourself and try to follow the **Getting Real Process** yourself. There's a chance you could find your way, though you may run into some dead ends without some guidance. After all, we are creatures of habit, and we prefer to take the path of least resistance. But less resistance doesn't usually get us what we want.

Option 3. Work with someone who does this for a living and has helped hundreds of people transform their lives. Get yourself the guidance of an expert who's been there.

If you're the kind of person who doesn't like to waste time, I invite you to go to www.RealTalkwithHilary.com and take my free **Real Talk Quiz.** This will provide some much-needed insight into the real (and likely heavy) cost of not speaking your truth out loud all these years.

Are you thinking maybe you will do this next week when you have more time? By next week, you and I both know there will be a new reason or excuse. Maybe you'll conveniently forget. (I sound like I'm talking about my old self.)

I love working with women like you. How do I know you? You're reading this book, aren't you? That tells me we must have a lot in common.

I was where you are now *for 12 years.* I wish there had been someone who could teach me the art of **Real Talk.** I would have saved myself 12 years of being miserable. I honestly only want what's best for all women. I love seeing women who feel happy and fulfilled instead of indignant and miserable. Being indignant and miserable comes with a big price tag; it costs us vitality, love, energy, and connections with others. Is the status quo really worth all of that?

I feel like I had to go through what I did so that I could help you get to your happy place. It gives me a sense of purpose to know that I can now help others "get real" faster.

Not long after developing my **Getting Real Process,** I met with my financial planner, and I wanted the meeting to be quick because I had another appointment.

"Why are you smiling?" I asked him impatiently.

 He was looking at my numbers. "You did it," he said.

"Did what?" I asked.

"You got what you wanted. Your retirement is set; you have savings. You are taking vacations, taking your daughter to Hawaii as you promised, and making more than you spend. You did it."

It took me a minute to register. *"You did it."* When it finally sunk in, I burst into tears and went around his desk to hug him.

I *really* had done it. I created the financial life I wanted.

I set myself free.

I wish the same for you.

So now, go take the **Real Talk Quiz;** it's kind of fun and eye-opening at the same time. It's also quick. Most importantly, it will show you how much you hold in and why you need to let it out.

One last thing; if you'd like to find out if my **Getting Real Process** can work for you, let's do some **Real Talk** together. Go to my website and book a no-cost Real Talk call — it's more like a conversation, and I promise you, there are no strings.

Thank you for reading this far. I hope you got something "real" out of this short book. Feel free to email me at hilary@ gettingrealwithhilary.com and let me know if you have any questions. I read and respond to all my emails.

Here's to *getting real.*

ACKNOWLEDGEMENTS

Without the guidance and support of so many people, this book would not be possible.

My parents – who always encouraged me to be my best. They believed in me no matter how I acted or what I thought. I love you both. I miss you, Dad.

My children – who encourage me every day to continue to do what I'm afraid to do, inspire others, and be a "cool mom."

My siblings – I am forever grateful to be part of the "Arnow Bunch." We are blessed.

My many mentors, angels, friends, and leaders at Landmark Worldwide – who taught me it was ok to speak up and that I truly have a miraculous life. Who taught me to let people know the real, creative, courageous me instead of hiding behind my pretending, pleasant phony self. That is how Getting Real with Hilary was born.

Friends and Family – for believing in me no matter what and not believing my disempowering victim stories.

Kathy Clabbe - Who introduced me to Lin and her Book to Business program while channeling during a tarot card reading of all things!

Lin Eleoff and her company, Book to Business – for your patience, wisdom, and amazing program that has birthed this book and taught me that I, too, have a powerful message and process that is needed and wanted in the world.

I am forever grateful and blessed to have you all in my life.

Hilary

ABOUT THE AUTHOR

Hilary Arnow Burns is the host and executive producer of the popular *Getting Real With Hilary Show,* a Radio/TV show featuring ordinary heroes who share extraordinary stories about life's challenges.

A graduate of the Wharton Business School, Hilary spent 30 years in the financial world before setting off to start her own business, dedicating her life to empowering women to speak their truth by implementing her unique "Getting Real" Process.

A speaker and author of several books, Hilary prides herself in being an entertaining and inspiring storyteller who uses her own daily life as an example of how a woman can go from feeling utterly miserable to joyfully fulfilled.

The mother of "two wonderful children" lives happily on the water in Connecticut.